MUMMIES

CATHLEEN SMALL

 Cavendish
Square

New York

CREATURES OF FANTASY

Mummies

BY

CATHLEEN SMALL

CAVENDISH SQUARE PUBLISHING · NEW YORK

Published in 2017 by Cavendish Square Publishing, LLC
243 5th Avenue, Suite 136, New York, NY 10016

Library of Congress Cataloging-in-Publication Data

Cataloging-in-Publication Data

Names: Small, Cathleen.
Title: Mummies / Cathleen Small.
Description: New York : Cavendish Square, 2016. | Series: Creatures of fantasy | Includes index.
Identifiers: ISBN 9781502618542 (library bound) | ISBN 9781502618559 (ebook)
Subjects: LCSH: Mummies--Juvenile literature.
Classification: LCC GN293.S63 2016 | DDC 393'.3--dc23

Editorial Director: David McNamara
Editor: Kristen Susienka
Copy Editor: Rebecca Rohan
Art Director: Jeffrey Talbot
Designer: Joseph Macri
Senior Production Manager: Jennifer Ryder-Talbot
Photo Research: J8 Media

The photographs in this book are used by permission and through the courtesy of: Fer Gregory/Shutterstock.com, cover; Andrea Izzotti/Shutterstock.com, 2; Andrea Izzotti/Shutterstock.com, 6; J.D. Dallet Therin-Weise/Getty Images, 8; Fedor Selivanov/ Shutterstock.com, 11; Werner Forman/Universal Images Group/Getty Images, 12; David L Ryan/The Boston Globe via Getty Images, 14; Werner Forman/Universal Images Group/Getty Images, 17; File:TUT-Ausstellung FFM 2012 47 (7117819557).jpg/Wikimedia Commons, 21; Columbia Pictures/Archive Photos/Getty Images, 22; Keystone-France/Gamma-Keystone via Getty Images, 24; Universal Pictures/Getty Images, 25; Daniel Simon/Gamma-Rapho via Getty Images, 26; Mohamed El-Dakhakhny/AP, 30; Ben Curtis/AFP/Getty Images, 33; GraphicaArtis/Getty Images, 34; Daniele Pellegrini / Science Source, 39; Ethan Miller/Getty Images, 40; ChinaFotoPress/Getty Images, 42; Adam Berry/Getty Images, 45; Veronique Durruty/Gamma-Rapho via Getty Images, 46; Eye Ubiquitous/ UIG via Getty Images, 49; Alexis Duclos/Gamma-Rapho via Getty Images, 50; Agung Parameswara/Getty Images, 51; Universal Pictures/Newscom, 54; File:Dagar, Desert Hawk No 15 Fox Features Syndicate, 1948.jpg/Wikimedia Commons, 57; Universal Pictures/Album/Newscom, 58; Hanna-Barbera Productions/Album/Newscom, 59

Printed in the United States of America

CONTENTS

INTRODUCTION

Mummies are sometimes, but not always, wrapped in linen cloths.

Since the first humans walked Earth, myths and legends have engaged minds and inspired imaginations. Ancient civilizations used stories to explain phenomena in the world around them, such as the weather, the tides, and natural disasters. As different cultures evolved, so too did their stories. From their traditions and observations emerged creatures with powerful abilities, mythical intrigue, and their own origins. Sometimes, different cultures encouraged various manifestations of the same creature. At other times, these creatures and cultures morphed into entirely new beings with greater powers than their predecessors.

Today, societies still celebrate the folklore of their ancestors—on-screen in TV shows and movies such as *Doctor Who, Once Upon a Time,* and *Star Wars,* and in books such as the Harry Potter and Twilight series. Some of these creatures truly existed, while others are merely myth.

In the Creatures of Fantasy series, we celebrate captivating stories of the past from all around the world. Each book focuses on creatures both familiar and unknown: the elusive alien, the grumpy troll, the devious demon, the graceful elf, the spellbinding wizard, and the harrowing mummy. Their various incarnations throughout history are brought to life. All have their own origins, their own legends, and their own influences on the imagination today. Each story adds a new perspective to the human experience and encourages people to revisit tales of the past in order to understand their presence in the modern age.

THE MUMMY MYTH

"For years I've wanted to write a book about mummies."
TESS GERRITSEN, BEST-SELLING AUTHOR OF *THE KEEPSAKE*

IMAGINE A CREATURE IN HUMAN FORM but whose flesh is largely invisible because the body is covered in strips of linen cloth from head to toe. Where the cloth has torn away, you can see glimpses of rotted, decaying flesh. This creature with its rotting skin must be dead—but then, it's not. It's alive, and it's coming after you!

This is not like any living creature *you* know—it's stronger and faster, and nothing you do seems to stop it! Knives and bullets don't stop it, so you try something else: you expose it to the searing heat of a roaring fire. No luck! Next, you lead it into a deep freezer, hoping to freeze the beast to death. No luck!

Opposite: The sarcophagus of Nitocris, believed to be the last pharaoh of the Sixth Dynasty of ancient Egypt.

Before you know it, the creature begins to throw things at you, but not by using its hands. It seems to be using its *mind* to do it! And then, it unleashes a swarm of bugs that seems to swallow you!

What is happening, you wonder? Well, my friend, it seems you've just met a mummy. And he's angry because you invaded his sacred resting spot when you were playing around with your friends, exploring that old cave you found.

So what can you do? Well, you've already angered the creature, so your best bet now is to try to understand what motivates him and what he wants so you can get out of this situation. Lucky for you, you've got this book to help you.

What Is a Mummy?

In reality, a mummy is simply a very well-preserved body. Mummies occur by natural means and as part of cultural rituals, and they are found all around the world—and no, they aren't *really* going to unleash a swarm of insects on you. That is, unless you believe the myth of the mummy.

What Is the Myth?

There is a certain allure to the idea of preserved bodies from a storytelling standpoint. We are used to thinking of dead bodies as either decaying over the years as they lie in their coffins or as being **cremated** and rapidly turned into a pile of ash. But if you introduce a mummified body into the mix—well, suddenly you've got some good storytelling material. The *what ifs* are endless. What if the person isn't *really* dead? What if the person could come back to life? What if the person set a curse upon their death? What if a human activated that curse? Suddenly, there's a story, and everyone loves a good story.

The myth of the mummy comes in part from humans' love of storytelling. In **oral tradition**, in literature, in theater, in film and television, and in art, mummies have been explored as central characters, and fantastic stories have been woven around the *what ifs*. But the myth of the mummy also comes right from the source: from the people who buried the deceased. In some cultures—most notably ancient Egypt—tombs of mummified persons were actually thought to be inscribed with curses warning intruders to stay away from the tomb. It's hard to know exactly what these curses said because they are written in **hieroglyphics**, but it's generally thought that they warned intruders not to disturb the tomb or its contents. Tombs, after all, contained great numbers of valuables, which were buried with the dead as part of Egyptian custom at that time.

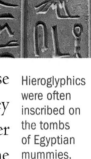

Hieroglyphics were often inscribed on the tombs of Egyptian mummies.

So combine those actual inscriptions with a love of storytelling, and suddenly you've got the myth: that these deceased individuals, so carefully preserved upon their deaths, can **reanimate** if disturbed and will hunt down and bring misfortune upon anyone who dares enter the tomb.

Then there's another layer: the fact that misfortune did indeed befall some archaeologists who uncovered tombs. Naysayers will call it nothing but coincidence, but it is true that in some cases, bad things happened to people who entered tombs. The best known of these stories involves the tomb of King Tut and the fact that eight people associated with the opening of the tomb experienced misfortune not terribly long afterward, but there are also other stories of people entering tombs and then suddenly falling ill and sometimes dying.

The scientific reasoning for these otherwise unexplained illnesses involves mold, fungus, bacteria, and the fact that these

pathogens tend to grow in sealed tombs, thus exposing those who open a tomb to potentially harmful substances. But those who subscribe to the curse of the mummy insist that misfortune befalls people because they violated the mummy's orders, not simply because they were exposed to dangerous mold.

As for the look of the mummy? Those linen wraps you see on mythical mummies do indeed have a basis in reality. Some mummies are created just from exposure to environmental elements, and they are not wrapped. However, in ancient Egypt, which is the culture best known for their mummification practices, deceased bodies were indeed wrapped in linen cloths when prepared for burial.

Creepy Real-Life Mummies

The Qilakitsoq baby from Greenland may have been buried alive because he had Down syndrome.

No doubt about it, the myth of the mummy is creepy. Certainly the curses reportedly written on Egyptian tombs add to the creepiness. But another factor adding to the overall unease of the myth of the mummy is that some famous real-life mummies seem to have died rather unpleasant deaths.

Take, for example, the Guanajuato mummies of Mexico. Several of these mummies are thought to have been buried alive in 1833 due to a cholera epidemic, and their mummified bodies still reveal expressions of horror on their faces. After visiting the tomb of these famous mummies, renowned science-fiction author Ray Bradbury said the experience "wounded and terrified" him—in fact, he was so affected that he quickly wrote the short story "The Next in Line," which takes place in the **catacombs** of Guanajuato.

Another famous mummy, the Qilakitsoq baby from Greenland, is thought to have been buried alive. He was a young Native child, discovered in 1972, who experts believe was placed into a grave with his dead mother in 1460 CE. The expression on the mummified baby's face is haunting, and it is thought that he was buried alive because he had Down syndrome (shown by DNA tests done on his mummified body) and thus would not be able to contribute meaningfully to the tribe after his mother's death.

Real-life mummies abound, and certainly, there are many stories about them. Entire books and encyclopedias have been written about real mummies. These stories are what help contribute to a good myth! Without the reality behind the myth, there would be no good tales, no creepy ghost stories, and no urban legends. Certainly, the myth of the mummy ranks high on the creepy scale where myths are concerned!

Don't Steal from a Pharaoh!

The myth of the mummy is closely related to the mummy's curse, which is also often called the curse of the **pharaohs**. The curse generally involves an individual who steals from a mummy's tomb being cursed by the mummy. In early days, tombs were prime territory for thieves, as they tended to be filled with riches and gifts to honor the dead. But as legend has it, the pharaohs did *not* like being stolen from, and sometimes the living had to go to extreme circumstances to protect the tomb's contents. Such was the case with pharaoh Ramses II. He was buried in the Valley of the Kings, but priests had to rewrap and move the body shortly thereafter to prevent looting. Three days later, he was moved yet again. But despite being moved twice, Ramses is actually thought to be the best-preserved Egyptian mummy!

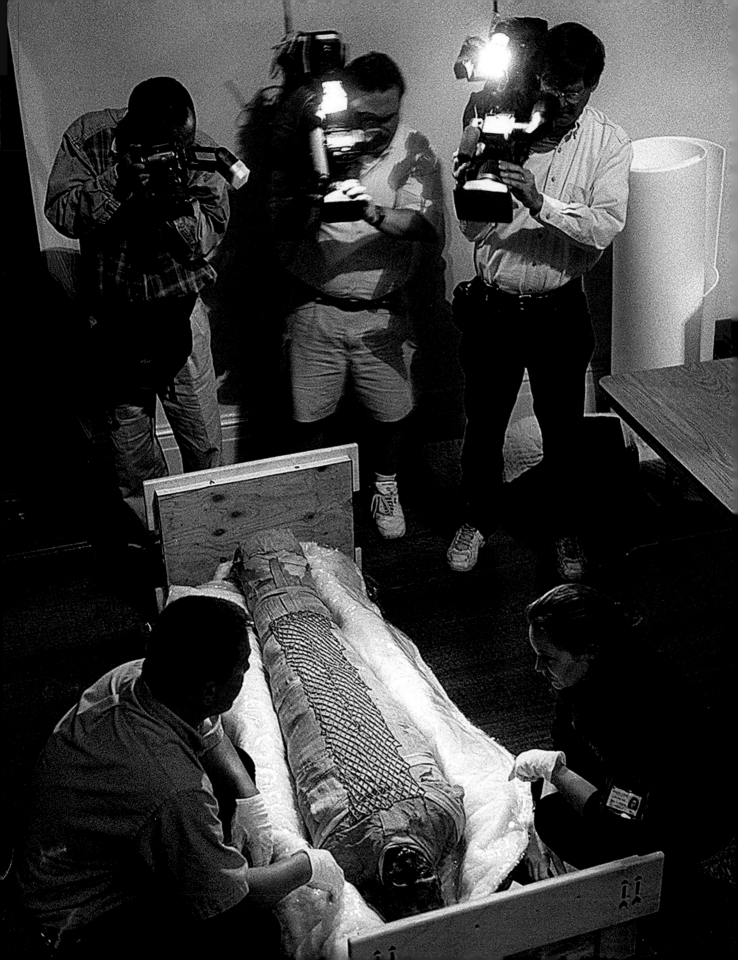

THE REALITY
BEHIND THE MYTH

"Two hundred and fifty mummies covered in gold. Something like this cannot be explained—mummy after mummy covered in shining gold."

ZAHI HAWASS, EGYPTIAN ARCHAEOLOGIST

MANY MYTHS START AS JUST THAT: STORIES. For example, there is no scientific evidence that such mythical creatures as elves, wizards, or trolls ever existed. Mummies, however, are different. We have absolute scientific evidence that mummies exist. They have become the stuff of myth and legend—countless stories have been woven around the mythical mummy's curse, for example—but that myth is grounded in an absolute reality. Mummies have existed for a very long time.

What Is a Mummy?

To understand the reality behind the myth of the mummy, you must first understand what a mummy is. You may have heard of

Opposite: A 2,500-year-old mummy was transported from Massachusetts General Hospital to the Museum of Science.

Egyptian mummies, and they are indeed real. But that's not the *only* type of mummy. *Merriam-Webster Dictionary* gives us two definitions of the word *mummy*:

(a) a body embalmed or treated for burial with preservatives in the manner of the ancient Egyptians

(b) a body unusually well preserved

The modern word is derived from Latin, Arabic, and Persian roots, all of which mean, basically, an embalmed corpse. Indeed, the ancient Egyptians embalmed corpses to preserve them. But the word *mummified*, a form of *mummy*, can also refer to a corpse that has been unusually well preserved by natural means. These bodies are often called spontaneous mummies.

Spontaneous Mummies

Spontaneous mummification occurs when the natural conditions in which the body lies are extremely hot and dry or extremely cold. It can also occur in areas with lower oxygen, such as peat bogs. Mummified corpses from as far back as 8000 BCE and the Bronze and Iron Ages have been found in bogs, but as recently as 2012, mummified bodies of World War II soldiers were found in bogs in Russia.

A well-known spontaneous mummy is George Mallory, an Englishman who ascended Mount Everest in the 1920s. He died on a climb in June 1924, but his mummified corpse wasn't found until May 1, 1999. Seventy-five years in the extreme cold and low oxygen near the summit of Mount Everest had preserved the climber's body.

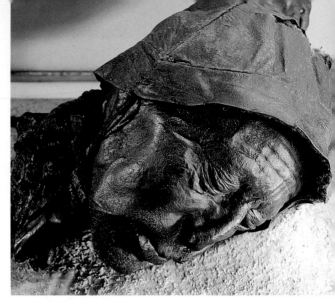

Another spontaneous mummy, Ötzi, was found in similar conditions in the Alps between Austria and Italy in 1991. He is believed to have died somewhere around 3200 BCE, and like Mallory, his mummified corpse was remarkably well preserved thanks to the altitude and cold in the mountains.

Tollund Man is a bog mummy. He is thought to have lived during the Iron Age, and his mummified corpse was found in Denmark in 1950.

In the United States, the oldest-known mummy was found in 1940 in a cave in Fallon, Nevada, by an archaeological team. Initially, the mummified corpse was thought to be less than two thousand years old. However, in 1996, an anthropologist reexamined the mummy and determined it to be from approximately 7420 BCE— roughly 9,400 years old! The amazingly well-preserved male mummy was found wearing a robe and leather moccasins and lying on a fur blanket. There was still skin on his back and shoulders, as well as a bit of dark hair on his head.

Spontaneous mummies have been found in Egypt, South and Central America, Asia, Alaska, the Alps, and northwestern Europe, among other places. Mummification could occur virtually anywhere with the correct environmental conditions.

Anthropogenic Mummies

While spontaneous mummies are a fascinating topic in their own right, what most likely inspired the mythical mummies are anthropogenic mummies. These corpses were deliberately mummified when living individuals embalmed the bodies of the dead and preserved them. When you think of King Tut and Egyptian mummies, it's anthropogenic mummies that you're thinking of.

Interestingly, though, the process of creating anthropogenic mummies was actually inspired by spontaneous mummies. Egypt is a very hot, very dry, sandy, desert environment, and before about 3500 BCE, when people died in Egypt they were buried in shallow pit graves, not in any coffin or sealed container. The sand and climate caused the bodies to naturally dehydrate, and they were preserved as mummies. This inspired the Egyptian cultural belief that a well-preserved body lives well after death.

Egyptians began to purposely embalm and mummify their corpses somewhere around 3400 BCE, and they continued to refine their techniques as the years passed. By around 2600 BCE, they had perfected their embalming techniques, although records from this time period are few. Archaeologists and other researchers have had to rely on tomb paintings and carvings depicting the mummification process, as well as a few spotty textual references from ancient Greek historians, most notably Herodotus (484 BCE–425 BCE), to piece together the procedure.

The Egyptians' mummification techniques were a closely guarded secret, but it is known that they removed the organs from a body, except for the heart (which they believed to be the center of the body and necessary for the afterlife). They washed the body with a blend of palm wine and spices. Then they dried the body and the organs, which were sometimes sealed separately from the body in **canopic jars** and sometimes wrapped and replaced in the body. The Egyptians preserved the body using a blend of minerals and oils. Evidence also indicates that they used **natron**, a salt, as a dehydration agent in their preservation efforts. In their refined mummification process, they also wrapped the body in linen cloth, which contributes to the image we have today of mummies being encased in long, gauzy strips of cloth. That cloth was then sealed with **resin** for further preservation. Finally, the mummified corpse was put in a coffin, which was then put in a sealed tomb.

The elaborateness of the mummification process depended partly on the individual's social status. Those of a higher social status were buried in more decorated, more carefully sealed tombs. So, some of the best preserved anthropogenic mummies from ancient Egypt are members of the higher social status, although eventually people from the Egyptian middle class were mummified as well. Commoners did not have the social status to be purposely mummified on their death; however, spontaneous mummification did still occur for these people because of the environmental conditions in Egypt.

Why Mummify?

So why all the interest in preserving bodies? The mummification process was long (lasting up to seventy days, historians believe) and complicated, so why did the Egyptians invest so much effort in it? Simply put, it was for religious and cultural beliefs.

The Egyptians believed in life after death. They believed that spirits lived well in the afterlife if their bodies were well preserved upon their death. The soul of each deceased individual was divided into several pieces, including the ka, ba, and akh. The ka represented the spirit that remained in the tomb with the mummified body, the ba represented the soul that left the tomb, and the akh was the combined spirit of ba and ka that traveled to the afterlife. They also believed that a deceased person's spirit (the ba) returned to and reentered its body to gain sustenance, so they thought bodies should be well preserved. They took great pains to refine their embalming

and preservation techniques so that natural decomposition would affect the corpse as little as possible—the goal was to keep the deceased person's body looking as close to lifelike as possible.

Within the layers of linen that embalmers wrapped around a corpse were amulets to guard the deceased person's spirit from evil. Magical words were sometimes written on the linen to ward off evil. Many of an individual's possessions believed to be of use to the person in the afterlife were also buried with the deceased. This included perfumes, food, soldiers or servants, and pets.

From Reality to Myth

So how did we get from Egyptian nobility, mummified and buried in elaborate tombs, to the mythical mummy wrapped in gauze bandages and bringing ill to those around him? The answer is likely the curse of the pharaohs.

Since the nineteenth century, it has been rumored that there is a curse of the pharaohs that will bring misfortune, illness, or death to anyone who disturbs a mummy's tomb or body. Indeed, there are some ancient tombs with curses inscribed on them. Some believe the curse in a magical sense—that indeed, a person who disturbs a tomb risks misfortune or worse—while others believe the curse in a scientific sense: that people entering a tomb are subject to bacteria or other substances that can cause illness. However, many believe the curse is simply a fun story with no basis in reality.

Whether or not the curse of the pharaohs is true, it has certainly inspired the modern myth of the mummy.

The Most Famous Mummy

Probably the best-known mummy to date is Tutankhamun, or King Tut, as he is more commonly known. King Tut was an Egyptian pharaoh who ruled around 1332 BCE. When he took the throne, he was about nine or ten years old, historians believe. He then married his half-sister and had two stillborn children with her. Historians believe that King Tut had some physical disabilities—they know he needed to use a cane, and evidence shows he had **scoliosis** and a deformity of his left foot, such as club foot, as well as a slightly cleft palate. He died at the young age of nineteen, and scientists believe that his ultimate death may have resulted from an immune system weakened by malaria. Controversy surrounds the theories about his cause of death, though. DNA evidence has shown that he did suffer from multiple strains of malaria, but there is also evidence that an infected fractured leg may have been the cause of death. Still another theory cites epilepsy as a possible cause. Still others think perhaps he was assassinated, since the region was in turmoil during his reign.

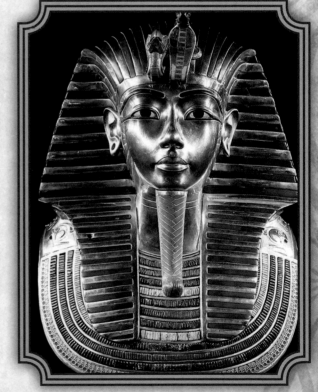

The golden mask of King Tut

Whatever the cause of King Tut's death, his remarkable tomb in the Valley of the Kings—a common burial site for Egyptian nobles—was discovered in 1922 by Howard Carter and George Herbert, also known as Lord Carnarvon.

3

SPECIAL POWERS

"Oh, look at this! Sons of the pharaohs! Give me frogs, flies, locusts, anything but YOU! Compared to you the other plagues were a joy!"

Dr. Terrence Bey, *The Mummy* (1999 film)

MOST CREATURES OF MYTH ARE IMBUED with special powers. Frankenstein's monster, for example, has great strength. Unicorns have healing powers. Fairies can fly and use magic. Genies can grant wishes. Mummies are no different—they, too, have powers. In fact, the power of the mythical mummy varies greatly depending on which myth you follow. To understand the mythical power of mummies, you must again look at the history behind them.

The Mummy Reality

Real mummies existed on almost every continent in some form or another—spontaneous mummies created by natural means have

Opposite: Books, television, theater, and film have all put a spin on the mummy's curse, such as in 1965's *The Curse of the Mummy's Tomb.*

been found all over the world. However, if there is one concentrated place where we think about mummies, it is undoubtedly Egypt. There are two reasons for this: First, many spontaneous mummies existed there because of the ancient Egyptians' burial practices and because of the climate conditions in the region. Second, the Egyptians' culture and religion drove them to purposely mummify their dead starting around 3400 BCE. This practice went on for a long time and is well documented in history. It drew the attention of people from around the world because, let's face it, it's a pretty interesting custom!

The Victorians in particular were fascinated by mummies. The study of mummies really began in the 1900s, and there are reports of Victorian "unwrapping parties," where people would gather to watch the unwrapping of a mummified corpse and the removal of the trinkets wrapped in the mummy's gauze. These unwrapping parties were generally done for private academic gatherings—rather than at, say, a house party—but nonetheless, they existed.

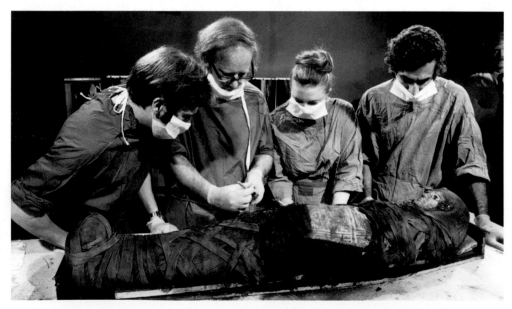

A mummy is unwrapped at Manchester University Medical School in the 1970s.

Although the Gothic period in literature occurred significantly earlier (in the mid-1700s), the Victorians still had a certain fascination with the **macabre**. Plus, Egypt was seen as exotic during that period—its people with their dark, swarthy complexions, different clothing, and mysterious religion and customs were somewhat fascinating to Europeans and Americans alike. It makes sense that when mummy studies began in earnest and Egyptian tombs were discovered, people reveled in the excitement of this strange-to-them custom. *What ifs* swirled—what if these remarkably preserved bodies could come back to life? What if their souls were still lurking around? What did they think about being disturbed?

Egyptian beliefs played into these *what ifs*. Remember, they believed the soul of the deceased split into a number of parts, two of which were the ka and ba. The ba, they believed, could leave the body after death and look for sustenance, but would return to the body at night. The ka, on the other hand, stayed with the body and got its sustenance from offerings left with the body. To progress into the afterlife, the ka and ba would combine into the akh. However, it wasn't that easy to become an akh after your death. If you were a pharaoh, you were pretty certain to become an akh, but if you weren't it got a little more difficult. If you weren't an akh, you wouldn't pass into the afterlife, and you risked reanimating as an undead. This is where the story of powers begins.

Reanimation and the Myth of the Undead

If a mummified corpse didn't become an akh and live eternally in the afterlife, it could rise from the dead. This occurred, the Egyptians believed, when the ka was not properly provided for. The ka would

be forced back into the mummified corpse and would rise from the dead to wander about in search of sustenance. The sustenance it searched for was reportedly human blood, animal flesh, or even fecal matter. The mummy would stop at nothing to be fed.

Playing off this Egyptian belief, people began to develop stories and legends about mummies, and about the powers they had when they rose from the dead. The stereotypical image of the mummy is a linen-wrapped corpse staggering around with arms out, moaning as it searches for nourishment.

In reality, the myths went much further than that. Like many mythical beasts, mummies were purported to be both strong and fast when hunting their prey. Their prey didn't have much of a way to defend themselves, because mummies were semi-immortal. They were nearly impossible to kill, because among their other

Mythical mummies are usually thought to be clothed in old linens and angrily in search of sustenance.

A mummified baboon from ancient Egypt

MUMMIFICATION: IT'S NOT JUST FOR PEOPLE!

The ancient Egyptians mummified people, of course, but you might not know that they also mummified animals for a variety of reasons. Sometimes pets were mummified and buried with their owners, but animals were also sometimes mummified and placed in tombs as gifts, offerings, or even food. Some animals that were worshipped while alive, such as Apis bulls and the rams of Elephantine, were mummified and buried as sacred animals.

powers, they were immune to disease, contaminants, temperature extremes, and lack of oxygen. Mummies could survive in regions of low oxygen—which makes sense, since spontaneous mummies can be created in low-oxygen conditions in certain regions! They could survive in extreme cold and harsh heat, which again makes sense, given that spontaneous mummies can be created in regions of extreme cold or heat. You can see how the reality of spontaneous mummies influenced their mythical powers.

Mummies also had supreme endurance—far more than a typical human. Not only were mummies immune to disease, but some could reportedly generate and manipulate disease—a great danger to the mummy's prey. Further, as the myth goes, mummies were able to suppress pain and were invulnerable to bullets and knife attacks.

Some mythical mummies were described as having powers of **telekinesis**. They could move objects simply by using their mind. Some were even thought to be able to control environmental elements, from the ground and water to insects, such as scarab beetles, locusts, flies, and moths. In other words, if you had **entomophobia**, you didn't want to run into a mummy!

According to Egyptian belief, if a mummy reanimated, it was single-minded in its purpose to drive away or destroy anyone who threatened the mummified corpse by invading its tomb. The reanimated mummy had supernatural strength. So basically, you had a very angry, very strong, very determined mummy who would stop at nothing to destroy whoever invaded its tomb—and as the myth grew and changed, mummies became not only strong and single-minded, but also capable of almost anything and vulnerable to almost nothing.

The Mummy's Kryptonite

Everyone has a weakness, even superheroes. Look at Superman: he could be stopped by a simple little element known as kryptonite. Mythical mummies were no different. It might *seem* impossible to kill something that's undead, but like anything else, mummies do have a weak spot. Their one weakness is fire. As legend has it, the resins and oils used to coat and seal the mummy's dressings are quite flammable, as was the linen itself, and thus the one way a mummy can reliably be killed is with fire.

This, of course, is the mythical belief. The ancient Egyptians had a slightly more realistic vision of how to kill a mummy: You had to destroy the corpse, erase any time the person's name was mentioned, and destroy any pictures or statues of the person. Only then, when the person was virtually erased from history, could you kill a mummy.

4

THE CURSE OF THE MUMMY

"As for anybody who shall enter this tomb in his impurity:
I shall wring his neck as a bird."

Curse carved into the tomb of Hermeru (2345 bce)

THE MYTH OF THE MUMMY IS LARGELY centered around the curse of the mummy or the curse of the pharaohs. Whether this curse is real or not depends on who you ask! But if nothing else, the supposed curse has lent itself well to the mythical mummy in literature, art, theater, and film.

The Beginning of the Curse

Although many believe that the mummy's curse began after the discovery of King Tut's tomb, in reality, the idea of the curse existed a hundred years before King Tut's tomb was opened. Egyptologist Dominic Montserrat found evidence that in

Opposite: The tomb of Queen Nefertari, wife of King Ramsis II.

a nineteenth-century London stage show, "mummies" were unwrapped onstage, prompting writers to create stories about mummies getting revenge. In 1869, Louisa May Alcott, now well known as the author of *Little Women* (published in 1868), published a short story called "Lost in a Pyramid; or, The Mummy's Curse," which deals with a stolen Egyptian **antiquity** that brings a curse upon the story's heroine.

Contrary to the belief of some, however, Alcott was not the first author to use the mummy's curse in her fiction. She was likely inspired by French author Théophile Gautier's 1840 story, "The Mummy's Foot," which also dealt with Egypt—more precisely, with the mummified foot of Egyptian princess Hermonthis.

There is some debate over whether Dominic Montserrat was correct in his claim that the mummy's curse did not originate in Egypt and that instead, it was the product of English literature and theater. In a *National Geographic* article by Brian Handwerk, Egyptologist Salima Ikram argues that some tomb walls in Giza and Saqqara contain evidence of written curses that threaten those who invade the tomb with "divine **retribution** by the council of the gods ... Or a death by crocodiles, or lions, or scorpions, or snakes."

Regardless of whether stories of the curse began in Egyptian tombs, on the London stage, in the pages of French and English literature, or elsewhere, it's undeniable that the story of the curse did *not* begin with the discovery and subsequent opening of King Tut's tomb. However, that is when the curse gained much widespread attention, and it is probably the best-known source of the myth of the mummy's curse.

The team in King Tut's tomb removes the lid of the sarcophagus in 2007.

King Tut and the Myth of the Mummy

On November 4, 1922, Howard Carter, a British archaeologist, was working with a team when they discovered the steps leading down to King Tut's tomb in Egypt's Valley of the Kings. Approximately three weeks later, Carter and his **benefactor**, Lord Carnarvon, entered the initial room of the tomb, which was composed in total of several rooms containing thousands of objects. The most important of these objects, of course, was the set of nested coffins, the innermost one made of solid gold, which contained the body of King Tutankhamen—or King Tut, as he is widely known. Carter and Lord Carnarvon found it on February 17, 1923, when they finally entered the boy king's actual burial chamber.

Lord Carnarvon was a wealthy Englishman who financed Howard Carter in his multiple attempts to locate King Tut's tomb. His given name was George Edward Stanhope Molyneux Herbert, and he was the Fifth Earl of Carnarvon, thus his more common moniker of Lord Carnarvon. He was an **aristocrat** and an amateur archaeologist, but his biggest role in the discovery of King Tut's tomb was offering financial backing to Carter. Much of the money that funded Carter's searches is actually reported to have come from Lord Carnarvon's wife, the wealthy Almina Victoria Maria Alexandra Wombwell.

Lord Carnarvon was present with Howard Carter at the opening of King Tut's tomb in 1922.

If you believe the curse of the mummy, then Lord Carnarvon should've kept to financing and avoided joining Carter as he entered the tomb. Just weeks after the two men entered the tomb that contained the three-thousand-year-old mummy, Lord Carnarvon died at age fifty-seven. Officially, he died of blood poisoning after a mosquito bite on his face became infected. However, several spooky events arose upon his death. It was reported that the lights in Cairo, Egypt, went out at the moment when Lord Carnarvon died, and reports surfaced that Lord Carnarvon's pet dog died at precisely the same time as her master did. However, whether these events were connected to a curse is debatable. Egyptologist Joyce Tyldesley mentioned both of these stories in an article she wrote for LiveScience.com, published in 2013 on the ninetieth anniversary of Lord Carnarvon's death. She said that in actuality, Lord Carnarvon's dog, Susie, died several hours after her master, and in her 2012 book, *Tutankhamun's Curse: The Developing History of an Egyptian King*, Tyldesley pointed out that power loss in

Cairo was quite common at that time, so the fact that the lights supposedly went out when Lord Carnarvon died wouldn't be particularly surprising.

However, Lord Carnarvon's death wasn't the only unfortunate event surrounding the opening of King Tut's tomb. It is reported that Howard Carter's pet canary was eaten by a cobra after the opening of the tomb, which believers of the curse see as noteworthy because the cobra is a symbol of the Egyptian monarchy.

Among others murmuring about a curse, Sir Arthur Conan Doyle, famous author of the Sherlock Holmes stories, supported the rumors surrounding Carnarvon's death. Gothic novelist Marie Corelli wrote of her own suspicions that those invading the tomb of the late king would run the risk of falling victim to a curse,

The Myth of Lord Carnarvon

The mummies aren't the only ones in this tale who've been spun into stories. Lord Carnarvon has regained attention as of late, thanks to the immense popularity of the BBC series *Downton Abbey*. The beloved series is filmed on location at Carnarvon's home in Hampshire, England, Highclere Castle, a massive estate that the current Lady Carnarvon estimates to have "between 50 to 80 bedrooms." Descendants of Lord Carnarvon still inhabit the estate, although the main house is in need of repair, so the family currently lives in another home on the property. Although the characters and storyline in *Downton Abbey* are reportedly fictional, it's widely believed that main character Lady Grantham is based on Lord Carnarvon's wife, Almina, and that other characters in the popular series were modeled after Lord Carnarvon's family.

citing an ancient Arabic text she possessed called *The Egyptian History of the Pyramids*, which reportedly stated that "secret poisons enclosed in boxes" would cause people who touched them to suffer. Corelli also reportedly informed the press that the tomb was inscribed with the words: "Death comes on wings to he who enters the tomb of a pharaoh," which is a section from the ancient Egyptian *Book of the Dead*—the name given to Egyptian **funerary** texts. The spells and illustrations that comprised the texts were written on papyrus and placed in a deceased person's tomb. However, that assertion was later determined to be false—the saying was *not* written on King Tut's tomb.

It's not surprising, though, that Corelli and others might've expected there to be a curse inscribed on King Tut's tomb. There *were* reportedly curses inscribed on other tombs, as Egyptologist Salima Ikram suggests. One such curse was found on the tomb of explorer Harkhuf and reads: "As for any man who shall enter into [this] tomb, ... [I will seize] him like a wild fowl; he shall be judged by the great god." And Amenhotep, the second king of Egypt's eighteenth dynasty, threatened that intruders to his tomb would "lose their Earthly positions and honors, be incinerated in a furnace in execration rites, capsize and drown at sea, have no successors, receive no tomb or funerary offerings of their own, and their bodies would decay because they will starve without sustenance and their bones will perish."

Regardless of the truth of the ideas spread by Doyle, Corelli, and others, the newspapers loved a good story and latched onto the idea of a curse. As Joyce Tyldesley commented, "Given the choice between focusing on the pretty average life of King Tut, a tomb they weren't allowed to see and a relatively uneventful

death, journalists can't be blamed for wanting to write about a mysterious ancient curse; no matter how unlikely its existence really is." Whenever anyone associated with the tomb experienced some sort of tragedy or misfortune, the media attributed it to the curse of the pharaohs. For example, in 1925, anthropologist Henry Field visited the tomb, and his house burned down shortly thereafter—and then was flooded after it was rebuilt. Sir Bruce Ingham, a friend of Howard Carter, was the recipient of a macabre paperweight made of a mummified hand and wrist wearing a bracelet marked with the words: "Cursed be he who moves my body. To him shall come fire, water and pestilence." Ingham's house later burned down twice. Egyptologist Hugh Evelyn-White, who was one of the first people to enter King Tut's tomb, reportedly committed suicide and wrote in his own blood, "I have succumbed to a curse." And Sir Archibald Douglas Reid, a radiologist, reportedly died just days after X-raying King Tut's mummified body in 1924.

In total, eight of the fifty-eight people who were present when the tomb was opened died within a dozen years, which believers cite as proof of a curse. Nonbelievers, of course, think it's all coincidence and that in any given group of fifty-eight adults, eight may die within a dozen years. Further, naysayers point out that a sealed tomb contains deadly fungus, molds, bacteria, and toxins that those who enter the tomb may be exposed to. Among other things, the ancient Egyptians placed fruits and vegetables in the tombs to nourish the deceased person's soul, and in the environment of the sealed tomb, those edible gifts eventually decayed and caused molds to grow.

Interestingly enough, if there really *is* a curse of the pharaohs, one would expect Howard Carter to be the most likely to be affected by it. After all, he is the man who relentlessly pursued the unknown location of King Tut's tomb and ultimately found and opened it. However, Carter lived to the respectable age of sixty-four, eventually dying of Hodgkin's disease nearly seventeen years after his monumental discovery.

The Modern-Day Myth

Whether or not you choose to subscribe to the idea of the curse of the pharaohs, the fact is that the curse is what most heavily inspired the modern-day myth of the mummy. That linen-clad, supernatural, risen-from-the-dead entity who exists in our current legend and lore came from the burial practices of the ancient Egyptians and became a prevalent part of modern mythology after the 1922 discovery of King Tut's tomb. The myth changes depending on the teller and the medium, but it bears all the hallmarks of the whispered stories of mummies risen from the tombs of the ancient Egyptians.

Egypt wasn't the only country to have mummies. This Incan mummy is from Peru.

5

MEETING THE MUMMY

"Reaching up, I pulled it down, believing it to be empty, but as it fell, it burst open, and out rolled a mummy. Accustomed as I was to such sights, it startled me a little, for danger had unstrung my nerves."

LOUISA MAY ALCOTT, "LOST IN A PYRAMID;
OR, THE MUMMY'S CURSE" (1869)

BECAUSE MUMMIES ACTUALLY EXISTED —and in fact still exist—people have encountered them for centuries. In many cases, these encounters haven't been in any way noteworthy. Mummies are on display at multiple museums, and crowds of people view them every day, and no misfortune befalls them. However, then there are the other stories, where those who come in contact with a mummified body suffer misfortune soon thereafter, causing us to wonder whether there really *is* a mummy's curse.

Mummies and Museums

Quite a few museums worldwide have collections of mummies and Egyptian artifacts for public viewing. Some noteworthy museums

Opposite: One of King Tut's four miniature coffins

The British Museum is home to many mummies, some of which are temporarily sent to other museums for display.

that do include the Egyptian Museum in Cairo, the British Museum in London, the Metropolitan Museum of Art in New York City, the Louvre in Paris, the Egyptian Museum and Papyrus Collection in Berlin, Germany, and the Museo Egizio in Turin, Italy. In addition to the Met in New York City, the United States offers several other smaller museums that have mummies and/or related items on display: the Oriental Institute at the University of Chicago, the University of Pennsylvania Museum of Archaeology and Anthropology in Philadelphia, and the Museum of Fine Arts in Boston.

It's not at all surprising that Cairo's Egyptian Museum would feature an impressive collection. Visitors can see mummies of numerous members of Egyptian royalty, and even King Tut's gold funeral mask.

The Egyptian Museum in Cairo reportedly has the largest collection of Egyptian art and mummies, but the British Museum in London follows in a close second with its collection. This, too, is not surprising, given that for a time Egypt was under British rule. The British Museum is home to more than a hundred mummies, many of which are on display to the public. The mummies are of varying ages but generally date back to around 3000 BCE.

Destroying History: Corpse Medicine and Social Events

For a time in the sixteenth, seventeenth, and eighteenth centuries, mummies were actually eaten as medicine. The flesh and bone was turned to powder and swallowed by Europeans, particularly members of royalty, priests, and scientists. Wondering how they got hold of these mummies to ingest their remains? **Grave robbers**, of course. There was a healthy market for corpses in those days. Aside from the supposed medical benefits of ingesting human flesh, bone, and blood, people believed that by ingesting the remains of a deceased person, they were also taking the deceased's spirit and strength.

When the Victorians developed an interest in Egyptian art, culture, and practices, this practice ended, but the destruction of valuable history did not—the Victorians took to hosting public unwrappings of mummies. However, this part of history isn't quite as sordid as it might sound. Although stories float around about these unwrappings or unrollings being social events, in reality they were more for study than for sport. They didn't happen in Victorian parlors, as some sources would lead us to believe. Rather, they happened in academic settings, and the primary goal was to study the body to further humans' knowledge of history, science, and culture. Remember, in the mid-nineteenth century through the early part of the twentieth century, researchers didn't have access to **CT scans** and other tools to analyze mummies. Unwrapping the corpses and studying them was the only way they could learn more about them.

Tomb Raiders

Grave robbing was a problem in ancient Egypt. Mummies, after all, were buried in tombs filled with their riches and earthly belongings—some of which were quite valuable. Stone tables and papyrus from thousands of years ago detail occurrences where tomb robbers invaded and attempted to rob graves in the Valley of the Kings.

An interesting cycle emerged: Grave robbers would loot a tomb for mummies and valuables, and then they would reuse the tomb to bury their own family … providing fodder for the next grave robber who came along.

It was, in fact, a grave robber who made what is thought to be one of the greatest tomb finds in history: a family of wildly successful grave robbers named Abdel Rassoul found a tomb containing the mummies of Amenophis I, Tuthmosis II and III, Set I, and Ramses I and III.

Originally, grave robbers were mainly Egyptians, but in the 1800s, tomb raiders from Europe began to arrive in Egypt in search of tombs and riches. It was quite a lucrative endeavor, as the Egyptian government didn't generally stop them from keeping what they found. In 1950, the government finally put a limit on how much treasure could be taken from a tomb, but it was the late 1980s before they really enforced it.

Whether through grave robbing, tomb raiding, or simply touring a museum, there has been no shortage of opportunities for people to view or come in contact with mummies. The only question is, will they suffer the curse?

Modern Mummies: Body Worlds

It might surprise you to hear that even in the developed world, a version of mummification still exists. The Body Worlds exhibit, developed by a German anatomist, is a traveling exhibition of human bodies and organs that are preserved by a technique called **plastination**. The bodies are placed in different positions to show how the body works and to demonstrate the effects of certain medical conditions on the body.

Although some think the exhibit is incredibly macabre, the reported purpose of the exhibit is to teach visitors about the human body. And no, the bodies weren't procured by grave robbers. Rather, they were donated to the exhibition by the individuals before their deaths.

And macabre though this exhibition might be, it's also wildly popular. The various Body Worlds exhibits have had more than forty million visitors—making them the most successful traveling exhibition in history.

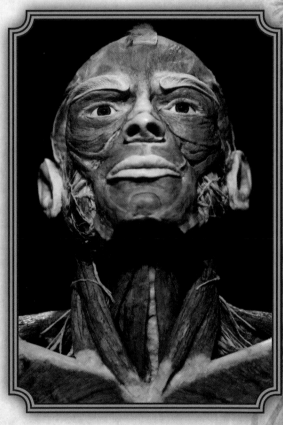

Body Worlds is a traveling exhibition of mummies preserved through plastination.

6

MUMMIES AROUND THE WORLD

"I had nightmares about dying and having to remain in the halls of the dead with those propped and wired bodies."

RAY BRADBURY, ACCLAIMED AUTHOR, OF HIS REACTION TO SEEING THE MUMMIES OF GUANAJUATO

ALTHOUGH WE MOST COMMONLY THINK of mummies as being Egyptian, in reality, mummies have been found all over the world. Basically, anywhere with an appropriate climate (extreme dry heat, extreme cold, or certain bog-like conditions) can produce a spontaneous mummy. Some of these mummies have elements of myth attached to them, and others are simply mummified corpses. But it's noteworthy that Egypt is far from the only place in the world where mummies are found.

Opposite: One of the San Pedro mummies from Chile

A Natural Mummy
in Native American Culture

Elements of Native American culture are heavily based on myth and legend, and one such myth was complicated by the discovery of a mummified body in 1932.

Certain Native tribes, including the Arapaho, Shoshone, and Sioux, include in their oral tradition stories of so-called "little people" who were between 2 and 3 feet (0.6 and 0.9 meters) tall. In some myths, these people were known as "tiny people eaters," and in fact, Shoshone legend speaks of these little people as "Nimeriga," who attacked the tribes with tiny bows and poisoned arrows. However, other tribes believed them to be magical spirits or even healers.

These supposed myths were established long before Columbus arrived and Europeans began exploring and settling America, and for a very long time they were thought to be just myth. But in 1932, gold miners Cecil Main and Frank Carr discovered a 14-inch (35.5 cm) mummy in a cave while they were using dynamite to try to blast for more gold. The mummy was remarkably well preserved, with even evidence of his fingernails still present, likely from having been sealed in a cave by thick rock, so scientists were able to test the body extensively. They believed that the mummy was that of a full-grown man, somewhere between the ages of sixteen and sixty-five—oddly enough, with a full set of canine teeth. Finally, proof of the "tiny people!" However, further testing indicated that the mummy may have been that of a diseased infant or child. The reality depends on which scientists you believe—no definitive answer has been given.

Whoever this mummified corpse was, he became known as the Pedro Mountains Mummy, or simply Pedro, and lore dictated that

anyone who possessed the mummy's body would have bad luck. It's unclear whether that was true for Leonard Waller, the last known owner of the mummy, who died in the 1980s. Pedro's mummified body has not been seen in decades, and it's not clear where it exists—assuming it even *does* still exist. Nowadays, of course, this would never happen. A mummified corpse would immediately become the property of a museum or university. But back when Pedro was discovered, there weren't so many restrictions in place. His mummified body was displayed in sideshows for years, and later it was sold to a Wyoming businessman, who eventually passed it on to Leonard Waller. Where it lies now is anyone's guess.

There are reports of cemeteries and burial grounds for pygmy races being found in Ohio and Tennessee as well, but these cemeteries and burial grounds contained skeletons, not well-preserved, mummified bodies like the one discovered by Main and Carr.

A Chinchorro mummy from Peru

Chinchorro Mummies

The Chinchorro people of southern Peru and northern Chile are thought to be the first people to create anthropogenic mummies, starting in around 5000 BCE and pre-dating even the ancient Egyptians! However, they were not the only people in Central and South America to adopt these practices—tribes from the Amazon and Andean regions did as well.

Fire mummies of
the Ibaloi tribe

FILIPINO FIRE MUMMIES OF THE IBALOI

The Ibaloi tribe in the Philippines had a unique and detailed months-long process for mummifying their dead. Scientists believe that starting around 1200 CE and lasting for about three hundred years (until Spanish colonization), the tribe created their mummification ritual, which involved the soon-to-be-deceased person drinking a very salty drink. After the person died, the body was washed and placed in a sitting position over a fire, which helped to dry the body externally. The body was dried internally by having tobacco smoke blown through the mouth. When the body was finally dry, herbs were rubbed onto the flesh, and the body was buried in a cave.

The mummification inspired the public to also refer to these Ibaloi as fire mummies. They are also sometimes called Kabayan mummies, after the region in which they were found in the Philippines. Nowadays, there are thought to be somewhere between fifty and eighty of these mummies remaining, mostly in caves in the Kabayan region, but also in a small museum in the region.

Smoked Bodies in Papua New Guinea

The Anga and Aseki people of Papua New Guinea have used a mummification process for about two hundred years to create the smoked bodies of the Morobe Highlands. This practice actually hasn't been legal since 1975, but it does still occur in some remote areas in the region.

The embalmer drains the body of fat and collects the drippings by cutting the feet, knees, and elbows of the corpse. The drippings are then smeared on living relatives, part of a ritual that is thought to transfer strength from the deceased person to his or her loved ones. The leftover grease is sometimes used as cooking oil to further transfer strength.

This smoked mummy from Papua New Guinea is thought to be almost four hundred years old.

To help preserve the corpse and prevent rotting, the embalmer then sews shut any bodily **orifices** and cuts off the person's palms, tongue, and the soles of their feet and presents these parts to the surviving spouse. The body is then smoked over a fire pit, much as meat is smoked in many other cultures. When the smoking process is finished, the body is placed in a cage of bamboo and placed on a cliff to act as a watcher or guardian for the village. The bodies are sometimes removed from the cage and brought down off the cliff for special events.

Although this mummification ritual may sound rather macabre, in reality, it is considered a great honor. It's interesting to note that while many myths of the mummy deal with anger and retribution, in this case, the mummy is seen as a protector of his or her people.

Buddhist Self-Mummification

In Japan, some Buddhist monks took mummification to a whole other level: they took it upon themselves to mummify their own bodies in a process known as *sokushinbutsu*. This incredibly detailed process, which was practiced in northern Japan between the eleventh and nineteenth centuries, wasn't terribly successful—of the hundreds of monks who were thought to attempt the feat, only twenty-four are known to have achieved it.

To achieve self-mummification, the monk would eat an extremely restricted diet of plant items, such as berries, pine needles, and tree bark. They slowly restricted the diet further, essentially starving themselves in a way that eliminated fat and fluids that typically cause a corpse to decay. Some even drank a tea made of a certain sap used to make lacquer; this sap was an **emetic** and also appears to have acted as an embalming fluid.

Once the monk felt he was ready to mummify himself, he would be sealed in a chamber with only a tiny opening for air. He would chant and ring a bell to signal those on the outside that he was still alive. When he stopped ringing the bell, the people on the outside would seal off the small hole into the chamber. The chamber would be reopened in about three years to see whether the monk was able to successfully mummify himself.

As this particular myth goes, if the self-mummification was successful, then the corpse would be dressed in robes, enshrined, and worshipped so that the living could await the monk's reawakening.

Crypt Mummies of Europe

Although many examples of mummification practices come from Native peoples, they were certainly not the only ones to create

mummies. In Europe, bodies were sometimes placed in **crypts** or catacombs and mummified in that manner—these mummies were likely spontaneous, brought on from the sealed environmental conditions of the crypts. The Capuchin Catacombs in Sicily, for example, contains mummified bodies from three centuries. Relatively nearby in Urbania, Italy, fifteen mummies resided at the Church of the Dead. Sommersdorf Castle in Germany also housed a number of crypt mummies, as did Dominican churches in Hungary and Lithuania.

Different Town, Different Myth

As many different places as mummies have been found, there are almost an equal number of myths. They share some similarities, of course—most involve some sort of reanimation of the corpse. However, they all reflect their different cultures and time periods as well. Some mummies are healers, some are guardians, and some are wrathful creatures seeking revenge on the living. Of course, as with anything, the myth evolves over time. After all, a great story has to keep up with the times, right?

7

MUMMYMANIA: THE MYTH TODAY

"You better think of something fast, because if he turns me into a mummy, you're the first one I'm coming after."

EVELYN CARNAHAN, *THE MUMMY* (1999 FILM)

MUMMIES STARTED OUT AS AN ACTUAL thing, and they still exist as such. Although anthropogenic mummification isn't common in *most* cultures, it does still exist in some, such as in tribes in Papua New Guinea and the Philippines. Spontaneous mummification, though, certainly occurs, perhaps most notably on places like Mount Everest, where it can take years to discover the bodies of deceased climbers, and when they *are* discovered—depending on the environmental conditions—the bodies are sometimes mummified.

Even more than actual mummies, the myth of the mummy persists. Perhaps this is because mummies are fun! The story of the mummy, the legend of the undead rising in pursuit of those people

Opposite: A shot from 1932's *The Mummy*, starring Boris Karloff

who have invaded its tomb—it makes for a good tale. Because of that, the myth of the mummy is ever present in our modern culture.

Mummies in Literature

Although there are reports of mummies in literature as far back as the late seventeenth century, the myth of the mummy first appeared in modern literature back in the nineteenth century, when Jane C. Loudon published the novel *The Mummy!* This theme persisted in later works. As you've read, Louisa May Alcott wrote the short story "Lost in a Pyramid; or, The Mummy's Curse." Sir Arthur Conan Doyle, who helped spread the idea of the curse of King Tut's tomb, wrote two mummy stories in the late nineteenth century: "The Ring of Thoth" and "Lot No. 249." Gothic novelist Bram Stoker, of *Dracula* fame, wrote a mummy novel entitled *The Jewel of Seven Stars* in the early twentieth century.

Mummies still feature in current literature. Phenomenally successful novelist Anne Rice published *The Mummy, or Ramses the Damned* in 1989. In 2013, the Egyptian Exploration Society and Jurassic London published *The Book of the Dead,* an anthology of nineteen original fiction mummy stories. So prevalent is the mummy in fiction that author Brian J. Frost has written an entire guide to mummy literature, in which he summarizes the plots of *five hundred* works of mummy fiction (along with 250 nonfiction books on mummies). It's safe to say, then, that mummies are exceedingly popular as a literary topic!

Mummies in Film and Television

Almost any topic that is popular in literature will also find popularity in other arts. Mummies are no exception. Before the

modern era, mummies did appear in some theatrical productions, but once film was developed, the myth of the mummy enjoyed even more success. Some silent films of the 1920s included mummies, and in 1932, *The Mummy* starring Boris Karloff premiered, launching the creature into more widespread fame. The writer of that film, John Balderston, was actually a journalist who had written about the opening of King Tut's tomb, and the film enjoyed great success. Universal Studios, which produced the film, played off the movie's success and released several other films featuring mummies in the 1940s and 1950s. The films were quite popular and they translated to television in the late 1950s, when so-called creature features became popular on American television.

Mummies appeared in comic books, among other literature.

Naturally, the success of the mummy as a movie icon meant the character featured in other successful ventures. Think about successful film franchises such as *Star Wars* and *Harry Potter* now—once a film becomes a smash, characters from that film appear in everything from trading cards to action figures to comic books. So, too, was the case with mummies—once they achieved success as characters in film and on television, mummy products began to appear everywhere.

However, the mummy isn't merely a popular character from the mid-twentieth century. Just like mummies in literature, mummies have remained popular in film and on television. Probably the most popular modern example is the 1999 film *The Mummy*,

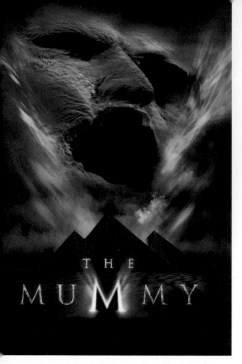

The 1999 film *The Mummy* was a box office smash.

starring Brendan Fraser. This film was somewhat of a remake of the 1932 film, but it spun in its own direction. The film was a smash, exceeding the studio's expectations for it, which led to sequels *The Mummy Returns* (2001) and *The Mummy: Tomb of the Dragon Emperor* (2008), a television series called *The Mummy: The Animated Series*, and a spinoff film called *The Scorpion King*. In addition to these films, Universal Studios opened a *Mummy* roller coaster at several of its theme parks.

While *The Mummy* and its related films have gained popularity, the myth of the mummy has also appeared in decidedly less popular films. A little-known film called *Monster Mash* featured the mummy in a **campy** role where deceased rock legend Elvis Presley is a mummy determined to make a comeback. Also, low-budget horror films such as 1981's *Dawn of the Mummy* often revisited the myth of the mummy.

The myth of the mummy lends itself well to all kinds of films, and naturally it falls neatly into the horror genre—in America and elsewhere. For example, *Tale of the Mummy*, released in 1999, is a British-American horror film. Hammer Films, a British production company, enjoyed several successful films featuring the mummy from 1959 to 1971.

Of course, no monster myth would be complete without being featured in the classic cartoon series *Scooby-Doo*. Mummies appear several times in Scooby-Doo cartoons, but perhaps most notably in the 2005 film *Scooby-Doo! in Where's My Mummy?*

This popularity of mummies in film does not appear to be ending either. As of late 2015, it's reported that Universal Studios is going to be launching yet another reboot of the *Mummy* series.

It's safe to say that the popularity of the myth of the mummy isn't waning, and why would it? The beauty of a myth is that it can endure and take on many forms. The main elements of the myth remain—the undead, a curse, revenge—but the story itself can change and include various settings and characters. Much like mummies themselves never die, the myth never has to die—it can continue in various incarnations for as long as people delight in the thrill of the undead.

Naturally, *Scooby-Doo* featured the mummy!

The Mummy Meets Camp

While the myth of the mummy can be frightening (with angry souls taking revenge on those who disturb them), it can also be delightfully amusing, with an element of the ridiculous. The 1955 Abbott and Costello film *Abbott and Costello Meet the Mummy* exploited this ridiculous side of the myth and is probably the most popular comedy-horror film featuring the mummy. The film follows the general mummy myth—a precious medallion is stolen from a mummy, and those involved in its theft later learn that it's cursed—but it quickly descends into the ridiculous. Lou Costello ends up eating the medallion in a hamburger, and he and Bud Abbott end up turning the mummy's tomb into a nightclub. The film also had success, proving that audiences enjoy all angles of the mummy myth.

GLOSSARY

antiquity Objects (usually of value) from ancient times.

aristocrat A person of nobility.

benefactor Someone who gives money to help another person.

campy A movie or television show that is so exaggerated or inappropriate that it becomes laughable.

canopic jars Pottery used by the ancient Egyptians to preserve and often store the internal organs of the deceased.

catacombs Underground tombs.

cremate To burn a body and turn it to ash.

crypts An underground vault or chamber in a mausoleum.

CT scan A computerized X-ray that shows cross-sectional images of a body.

emetic A substance that causes vomiting.

entomophobia The fear of insects.

funerary Associated with funerals or burials.

grave robbers People who broke into tombs or graves to steal bodies or valuables.

hieroglyphics A written language consisting of pictorial characters.

macabre Gruesome, horrifying.

natron A salt substance used in embalming practices in ancient Egypt.

oral tradition Cultural information and stories passed from one generation to another by oral storytelling.

orifice An opening on the body such as the mouth or nose.

pathogen Something that causes disease.

pharaoh The title for an ancient Egyptian ruler.

plastination A preservation technique in which water and fat in body tissue are replaced by a plastic polymer.

reanimate To come back to life.

resin A brittle solid usually used as a polish or varnish for materials such as stringed instruments and floors.

retribution Punishment for wrongdoing.

scoliosis A condition causing curvature of the spine.

telekinesis The use of the mind to move objects.

To Learn More About Mummies

Books

Cardin, Matt. *Mummies Around the World: An Encyclopedia of Mummies in History, Religion, and Popular Culture.* Santa Barbara, CA: ABC-CLIO, 2015.

Hart, George. *Ancient Egypt.* New York: DK Eyewitness Books, 2014.

Putnam, James. *Mummy.* New York: DK Eyewitness Books, 2009.

Website

Ancient Origins

www.ancient-origins.net

This website is chock full of information about ancient peoples and civilizations, and features many articles about ancient Egypt and mummies from different regions.

Video

"Mystery of the Black Mummy – Ancient Mysteries"

www.youtube.com/watch?v=CMIsLaSiNFs

This documentary covers the discovery of a mummy in Africa that suggests the ancient Egyptians weren't the first to mummify their dead.

BIBLIOGRAPHY

"Ancient Egyptian Book of the Dead." *The British Museum.* https://www.britishmuseum.org/pdf/3665_BOTD_schools_Teachers.pdf.

Asher, Lara. "Oldest North American Mummy." *Archaeology.* Sept/Oct 1996. http://archive.archaeology.org/9609/newsbriefs/nevada.html.

Bradbury, Ray. "Ray Bradbury Stories." *ePubsBook.* http://www.epubsbook.com/2015/4010_2.html.

Broder, Jonathan. "Egypt Has a Long History of Grave Robbers." *Fox News.com.* May 18, 2000. http://www.williamtolan.com/fno/EGYPT/story5.htm.

Davis, Lauren. "The Gruesome and Excruciating Practice of Mummifying Your Own Body." *io9.* Feb 4, 2014. http://io9.com/the-gruesome-and-excruciating-practice-of-mummifying-yo-1515905564.

"Egypt: The Curse of the Mummy." *Tour Egypt.* http://www.touregypt.net/myths/curseof.htm.

"Exhibitions." *Body Worlds.* http://www.bodyworlds.com/en/exhibitions/past_exhibitions.html.

"Fire Mummies of the Philippines." *Atlas Obscura.* http://www.atlasobscura.com/places/fire-mummies-of-the-philippines.

Hawass, Zahi. "Secrets of the Valley of the Kings." *Official Website of Dr. Zahi Hawass.* http://guardians.net/hawass/Press%20Releases/secrets_of_the_valley_of_the_kings.htm.

Holloway, April. "The Mummies of Qilakitsoq and the Inuit Baby That Captured Hearts Around the World." *Ancient Origins.* http://www.ancient-origins.net/ancient-places-americas/mummies-qilakitsoq-and-inuit-baby-captured-hearts-around-world-001325.

Stewart, John. "Curses! Fungus Dispels the Myth of King Tut's Tomb." *Los Angeles Times.* July 30, 1985. http://articles.latimes.com/1985-07-30/news/mn-3981_1_moons-in-one-month.

Tyldesley, Joyce. *Tutankhamun's Curse: The Developing History of an Egyptian King.* London: Profile Books, 2012.

Weiser, Kathy. "Wyoming Legends: Little People & the Pedro Mountain Mummy." January 2014. *Legends of America.* http://www.legendsofamerica.com/wy-littlepeople.html.

Index

ABOUT THE AUTHOR

Cathleen Small is an author and editor who has written numerous books for Cavendish Square Publishing. She lives in the San Francisco Bay Area with her husband, where she is "mummy" to her two sons, one pug, and two cats.